Early Travel

Bobbie Kalman

The Early Settler Life Series

Crabtree Publishing Company

To my Mother, with thanks for her support and belief in us

Special thanks to *Lori Pattenden, Nancy Cook, Kathleen Scherf, Rosemary McLernon, Wally D. Bonner and Joanne Green.*

Cataloging in Publication Data

Kalman, Bobbie, 1947 –
   Early Travel

(Early settler life series)
Includes index.
ISBN 0-86505-007-4 hardcover
ISBN 0-86505-008-2 softcover

1. Transportation – History. I. Title. II. Series

HE 152. K 34   380. 5'09   C 81-094759-5

350 Fifth Ave, Suite 3308
New York, NY 10118

R.R. #4
360 York Road
Niagara-on-the-Lake, ON
Canada L0S 1J0

73 Lime Walk
Headington, Oxford OX3 7AD
United Kingdom

Contents

Early explorers traveled across the ocean to discover new land. John Cabot, his son and his crew sighted Newfoundland in 1497.

Pioneers traveled here from Europe to find new homes. These emigrants say goodbye to friends and family for the last time.

Why did the early settlers travel?

The pioneer's journey to the new homestead was usually a long one. After a stormy ocean voyage, most new settlers also had to travel inland by boat. After that part of the journey was over, many settlers, such as the family above, traveled on land by covered wagon.

Settlers traveled to visit relatives and friends in other towns and cities. These boys are happy to see their aunt again.

Many of the settlers and native people took part in the fur trade. They traveled to trade furs for supplies.

Settlers traveled from their farms to nearby villages. They bought supplies at the general store, ground their grain at the mill and came to worship God at the village church. These settlers built their church near a river so that they could reach it by boat.

These men are voyageurs. They work for a fur-trading company. They travel far to trading posts delivering furs and supplies. Most of their trips are made by birchbark canoe. When they come to land, the men must carry their canoes and supplies across the portage.

On foot and by canoe

Some of the first settlers who came to the New World were explorers who later returned to their homelands. Some stayed and made their living by trading for furs with the native people. These early fur traders either traveled through the bush on snowshoes or they collected their furs by canoe.

The early settlers traveled by boat as much as they possibly could. Travel on land was long, tiring and sometimes next to impossible. There were no roads. The earliest means of water transportation was the canoe. *Dugout* canoes were made of half logs of pine or basswood, scooped into hollow shells. Dugout canoes could glide through the water with hardly a sound. Hunters could sneak up on animals.

Portage your birchbark!

Birchbark canoes were better for traveling long distances. Because they were light in weight, they were fast and easy to carry. Travelers carried their boats between bodies of water. This route was called a *portage*. Gear and supplies were fastened onto the backs of people by a *tump line* which was strapped across the forehead.

Some of the *voyageurs* (people who made long canoe journeys transporting goods) could paddle a stroke a second and keep going as many as eighteen hours a day. Some birchbark canoes were large enough to hold sixty people and a lot of cargo. Birchbark canoes were made without nails. The birchbark strips were sealed and waterproofed at the seams with pine gum. They rarely leaked.

In this old picture men are stripping the bark from the trees. The bark will be used in making the outer shell of the canoe. Birchbark strips were also used as torches to aid travelers at night.

The native people invented the canoe. The native people in the 1865 photograph below have placed sheets of birchbark inside a framework of poles. The wooden ribs, lying on the ground, will next be placed at intervals along the bottom of the canoe. The birchbark will be attached to the ribs.

Saying goodbye to relatives and friends was a heartbreaking experience. Many of these people never saw each other again. A new life in those days meant giving up the many people you loved forever.

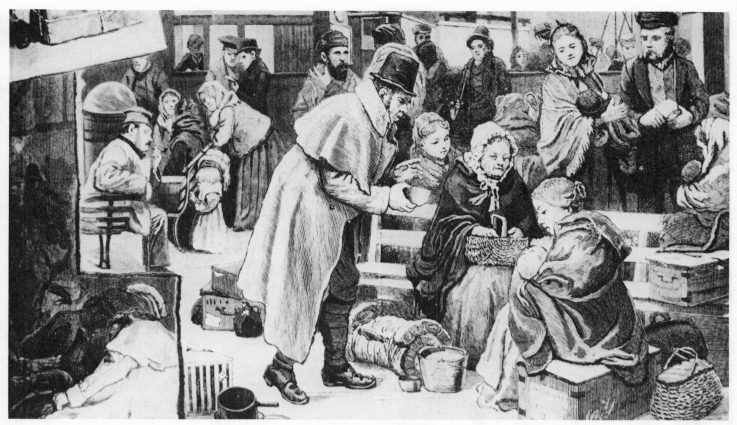

These hopeful emigrants think they are leaving their troubles behind on this dock. Little do they know that a living nightmare awaits them on board ship.

A better life in the New World

Most of the settlers who came to the New World from Europe came here in the last four hundred years. Some came as explorers, some came for the fur trade, some came for religious reasons, but most left their old countries for the same reason. They wanted to make better lives for themselves and for their families.

Many people, few jobs

In the early 1800s many Europeans had no jobs. Thousands of people moved to the cities. The cities became overcrowded. There were not enough jobs for everyone. Many people in the cities had no hope of finding work.

The situation in the country was not much better. Many farmers worked for large landowners. They paid the landowners rent for small areas of land. They then farmed that area and made a living from it. More and more large landowners, however, felt they could make more money farming all their own land themselves. The small *tenant* farmers were left without land, homes and jobs.

Famine and war

There was a famine in Ireland which left many people without food to eat. People were starving. Thousands of people had to leave their homes to find a new life.

Britain and France were at war with each other for many years. The war came to an end in 1815. When all the soldiers returned home they found that there were not enough jobs for all of them. People had to leave their homes. North America offered a great hope to Europeans. People felt they had a future in the New World. However, most did not realize the difficulties that lay ahead!

The Liverpool liars

Those who made the decision to leave their countries either bought tickets ahead, or made their way to the docks. Many left from Liverpool, England. Those who did not have tickets were often cheated out of their money by *emigrant runners* who sold them false tickets. Many people were charged much higher prices by these dishonest men.

People were crammed into tiny bunks, such as the ones in this picture. As many as six people had to share two of these little cubbyholes. If people were friends at the beginning of the voyage, most often they disliked each other by the end of it.

The captains of most ships ordered their passengers to go up on deck at least once a day, no matter how sick they were. Fresh air seemed to help the spirits as well as the lungs.

Terrible conditions at sea

Ships came to Liverpool carrying timber and furs from North America. These cargo ships then returned packed with people. They were roughly built, cold and dirty. The captains of these cargo ships grew greedy. They crammed their boats so full that the conditions on board were inhuman. Extra bunks were put in to make room for even more passengers! Almost all the immigrants to the New World traveled there under these conditions. Only a small number were able to afford a first-class voyage. About two thousand people were crammed into a small boat. Today, the same two thousand people would cross the ocean in a ship ten times the size of the one leaving Liverpool. Imagine sharing a large cabin with two thousand people! Wouldn't it make you want to face a potato famine instead?

The crews of the ships were often mean. They took pleasure in beating people up. They cheated passengers out of money and belongings. They made fun of the suffering of the passengers.

The emigrant travelers were given very little food. Often the meat they received had maggots in it. The passengers did their cooking on small stoves in the *hold*. (The hold is the cargo area at the bottom of the boat.) Sometimes they were lucky if they could cook at all. Once the ship hit a storm, all hope of cooking was gone. The ship would be tossed high on the waves. Everything and everyone inside the ship would be thrown from one end of the hold to the other.

Wet, sick and starving

In one case, the entire voyage was stormy. People nearly starved. They were drenched to the skin from the water that came in through the *hatches*. (The hatch was an opening on the deck over the hold.) Many people came down with diptheria. The epidemic spread through the ship, as people were too weak to fight off the infection. Sometimes entire families died on board without ever reaching land.

Those who were alive nearly went mad from their experience. They ranted and raved about the "watery grave" they were all headed for. They were not far wrong. If the ship did sink, there were only a few lifeboats on board. Fear was a large and real part of every ocean crossing.

Once the immigrants were examined by a doctor and found to be in good health, they often waited in boarding houses until they were ready to travel inland. They then had to find transportation to their new homesteads. The later newcomers were lucky enough to travel west by railroad. However, the earlier settlers had to make long, tiresome journeys by water and land. This wagon is loaded with the belongings of several families. These people are heading to the nearest boat, which will carry them on the first part of their long journey. From there, they might travel by coach, wagon, another boat, or even on foot. It will be weeks before they will be able to call any place "home".

Air out the problems

Some voyages were a little more pleasant than others. If the weather was not too bad, people could go up on deck and at least breathe some fresh air. Most captains ordered all the passengers on deck at least once a day to air their lungs and their clothes, no matter how ill they were. Fresh air helped to restore the spirits and prevent diseases on board. It was amazing that people survived the trip, with all the bad food, lack of clean air, seasickness and disease. Some people had broken bones from being tossed around on the ship so much. Babies and small children often did not survive.

The tell-tale tongue

When the ship landed, a doctor came on board to decide who was sick and who was well. Often the diagnosis was made by whether a person had a "furry tongue" or a "clean tongue". The people who had furry tongues were not allowed to stay. Many people had to face the same awful journey back to Liverpool again! Only this time, there was no hope at the other end! Those who were allowed to stay faced at least another month of pain and suffering traveling to their new homesteads.

Before the coming of the railroad, the journey was usually a very long one. A new immigrant would have to travel by boat, by wagon and on foot to get to the new homestead.

Boats galore!

Many of the early settlers made their homesteads near rivers or lakes. That way they could go to market, to the mill, to the store and to church by boat. Even before the immigrants became settlers they had to travel to their new homes. Much of the journey was made by boat.

Canoes were the earliest boats used. Pioneers learned how to make canoes from the native people. Canoes were light and could be carried across land to other bodies of water. However, for longer trips, canoes were not very comfortable or safe.

People used bateaux, flatboats, rafts, sailboats, houseboats, horseboats and keelboats for travel and transportation. Steamboats made water travel much more fast and efficient. Many of the biggest early cities grew up around lakes and rivers because no form of land transportation was as good as travel by boat. Roads were usually muddy and rough. The coming of the railroad helped to develop inland cities, but even today, port cities continue to be very important. Water is still the best way to transport goods to and from many locations.

Dangerous waters

Travel on the inland lakes and rivers was often as dangerous as coming across the ocean. Sudden gales overturned many sailboats. Some boats ran aground on sandbars or on large rocks hidden in the water. Because the early boats were powered by the wind or by rowing, most voyages took many days or even weeks to complete. The passengers could always look forward to getting drenched by waves or sudden storms.

There were stories of dramatic rescues on land and water. One story told of a sailboat named *Jeanie Johnson* which sunk on its way from Quebec to Hull in 1858. *Harper's Weekly,* an old newspaper, reported that the boat's owner and family were headed for market with a boatload of goods when the boat was hit by a

Because most of early travel was by water, the whole family had to know how to handle a boat. This young boy is learning how to sail. He is climbing the rigging to see what is in the water ahead.

The sinking of the Jeanie Johnson.

It was difficult to sail to market on a half-frozen lake. These settlers are stuck on a huge piece of ice. They are working

sudden gale. Everyone in the boat climbed up to the maintop and there they sat hanging on for several hours. They were rescued by the *Sophie Elizabeth*. The captain, crew and whole family arrived home safely. However, they did not make it to market!

Home by bateau

Many new settlers traveled to their new homesteads by bateau. The bateau was a large, flat-bottomed sailboat about twenty to thirty metres long and three metres wide. If there was no wind, the bateau had to be moved along by poles. Everyone sat on benches on the deck. There was no shelter against bad weather. At night these boats pulled up to shore and the passengers often slept under the open sky. A few inns were along the way, as well as farmers' houses, but most new settlers could afford neither. Many of the early settlers were taken to their new homesteads by bateau. Few arrived in good health.

This early type of bateau is being loaded with goods for market. It is low tide. As the water gets higher, the boat will be pushed farther in and the crew will prepare to sail.

hard to free themselves. They want to be among the first to reach the city market. What do you think their chances are?

Many new settlers arrived inland by bateau.

Traveling upstream was a very difficult task. These men have to pull their boat along from the shore. The rope is attached to the boat. If the current is too strong, the men on shore have to grab bushes and trees to prevent themselves from being dragged backwards by it. The trees act as a series of anchors.

Upstream the hard way

River travel was as challenging as travel on the lakes. The boats often hit snags. Logs stuck out of the water in the shallower areas. Traveling the rapids was the most dangerous part of river travel. The boats could be overturned or smashed on the rocks. The choppy currents of the rapids caused many passengers to fall overboard.

Going upstream against the river current was particularly tricky. Few of the early boats could manage this without the help of people outside of the boat. When a group of people wanted to travel upstream, some of them had to go onto the shore and pull the boat by rope against the current from there. The men on shore held onto the rope and moved from bush to bush, holding onto the bushes as they went. The bushes were like anchors, keeping the boat from going backwards. Using a rope to pull the boat was called *cordelling* and using the bushes to keep the boat from sliding back was called *bushwacking*.

Keelboats made upstream travel much easier and more enjoyable. The fiddler kept the passengers and crew sailing in tune!

Fiddling the keelboat

Keelboats solved the problems of traveling upstream against the current. The keelboat was pointed at both ends. The middle section contained the mast and sails. There were benches for rowers at the *bow* or front of the boat. At the *aft* or back of the boat, there was a raised stand from which the steersperson controlled the *rudder* which steered the boat. The sails and oars were used when the boat was going downstream.

Going upstream was a different story. The crew *walked* the boat upstream. Small rungs of wood were hammered to the walkway which ran along both sides of the boat. The crew stood at the bow and faced aft. They dug their poles into the bottom of the river. They placed the other end of the pole against their shoulders and walked along the rungs pushing on the pole. The boat moved as they walked. When they reached aft, they returned to the bow and started all over again. A fiddler kept the walkers in step and in good spirits.

This small ferryboat is being pulled across the river by a rope on pulleys. A man with an ox-cart waits for its return.

Horseboats were a great idea at the time. The horses turned the wheel that made the boat go. However, horses got tired, as people did. A new source of energy was needed to allow boats to travel under all kinds of conditions.

Tempers are raging at this ferry gate. The wagons in this old picture are loaded with the goods that were just unloaded from the large ships in the background. The drivers are in a hurry to get the new supplies home.

Crossing without a bridge

When pioneers traveled by land and came to a river, they faced a problem. Because there were few bridges, they had to walk along until they came to a shallow part of the river and then cross, or they found the nearest ferry operator to get them and their wagons across. Ferries were like huge rafts which were pulled across from one side of the river to the other by means of a rope and pulleys. A gangplank at both ends allowed the horses to pull wagons on and off the ferry.

Ferry operators grew rich quickly because the pioneers had no choice but to use their services. They were often able to charge any price they wished!

True horsepower

All of the early boats required windpower, or personpower. Travel by water was slow and difficult if the wind and current were against the traveler. It was necessary to find better means of water transportation. Paddle boats were invented. A large wheel was used to push the boat forward. Four horses turned an upper wheel on the deck, which turned a shaft, which turned the paddlewheel. The idea was good, but the source of energy was not efficient. Just as we are searching for new sources of energy today, the pioneers searched for new sources of energy to make their lives easier. The source they found was steam!

More efficient steampower

James Watt was a Scottish inventor. Even when he was a young boy his mind was occupied by thoughts of science. His parents and friends thought he was lazy. He didn't speak or read much. He spent hours playing with a kettle. He took the lid off and put it on again. He held a cup or a silver spoon over the steam. He watched how the steam rose from the spout into the cup or spoon. As soon as it hit the cold surface of the cup or spoon, the steam joined with other drops of water already formed there. The steam condensed or changed into water. Watt's experiments as a young boy helped him to invent a better steam engine when he grew up.

Years later as Watt was repairing a steam engine, he noticed something very important. The engine was losing most of its steam as it worked. The steam created the power to make the engine go, so losing steam meant losing power. Watt invented a new engine with a separate condenser. By using a separate condenser, none of the steam or power was lost. In the next few years Watt improved his engine even more. Watt's engine was the best steam engine money could buy in the 1800s. It was the engine Robert Fulton used when he built his first steamboat in 1807.

James Watt spent many of his young days playing with steam. His play led to interesting new discoveries about steam later on.

The Accomodation *was the first steamboat to navigate on the St. Lawrence. It was built in 1809. It was slow, but it did attract quite a few regular customers.*

The Walk-in-the-water *was Lake Erie's first steamer. It serviced Detroit, Windsor, Chatham, Black Rock and Buffalo, where it was wrecked in 1821.*

Fulton steams ahead

Robert Fulton was also an inventor. He was interested in designing canals, canal boats and submarines. He wanted to make it easier for people to travel. Another man, Robert R. Livingston, wanted to build a steamboat but did not know how to go about it. He talked Fulton into designing and building a steamboat. Fulton bought one of Watt's engines and set about building a steamboat that would improve water travel for the settlers. The *Clermont* was built in 1807. It was not the first steamboat in the world, but it worked well and made money for its owners.

Many of the earliest steamboats also had sails. That way they could be operated by wind, as well as by steam. Some steamboats had their paddlewheels at the side of the boat. They were called *sidewheelers*. Those which had their wheels at the back were called *sternwheelers*.

Noisy, damp and dangerous

Steamboats were not popular for quite a while. People were afraid of falling over-board because there were no safety railings. The boats were smelly and noisy, but most of all, they were new and people did not trust them. People in those days were not used to change as we are today. Many early steamboats blew up because the engineers did not know the limits of steam. If the fire was too hot and more steam was produced than was needed, the boiler blew up like a bomb.

Steamboats announced their arrival by a cannon shot fired from the deck of the boat. Many people reported that steamboats had curious middle-of-the-night arrival and departure times. One can imagine how many people fell out of bed from fright on hearing the middle-of-the-night cannon blasts. People who were brave enough to try early steamboats did not have many good things to say about them.

One man described his voyage on an early steamboat in the following words:

> *"Never in my life have I suffered more severely from the jolting, tossing, rolling and heaving...."*

Another said his cabin was "cellar-like, damp, cold and cheerless as a hole". The meal on board ship was also as bad as the rest of the voyage. The food was prepared by dirty hands. It was greasy and looked and smelled awful. Only a few of the passengers could bring themselves to eat it. It was not surprising that many people were suspicious of steamboats. The few who tried them probably told many about their bad voyages.

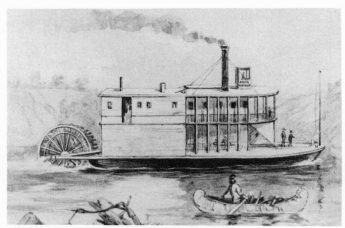

The Anson Northrup, *later known as* The Pioneer, *arrived in Fort Garry from Minnesota in 1859. It was taken apart, portaged and put back together at Red River.*

The Caroline *was set on fire by rebels in 1837 and sent crashing over Niagara Falls in a blaze of glory.*

Gambling was a popular activity on many boats. There were card games, board games and bets of all kinds. Steamboat races always provided good odds.

The parlors of the later steamships were grand. Traveling became a luxury when one could afford passage on such a boat.

Luxury on board

Steamboats became popular near the middle of the nineteenth century. More and more people traveled on them. The later steamboats were like luxury liners. The cabins were carpeted, fine dishes were used at meals, and musicians played for the entertainment of the passengers. Gambling was a popular part of the entertainment and a big business for the gamblers.

The later steamboats offered pleasures such as great food, great music and a comfortable voyage. These passengers enjoy reading, listening and talking to friends.

Everyone gathers on deck to cheer for the winning boat – their own!

Some of the steamboat races were over three days long!

Risking a blow-up

The fires are burning. The ship speeds ahead. The engineer in front wonders if the engines can take so much heat.

There was always a risk in traveling by steamboat. Even though the later steamboats were so comfortable inside, the engines were far from perfect. We hear about a lot of plane-crashes today. In the 1800s there were many steamboat blow-ups. One of the reasons for these blow-ups was that the captains and crews could not resist challenging other steamboats to races. Some of the races were many days long. The engines below had to work overtime to make the boats go faster. When too much steam was produced, the engine blew up like a bomb. Newspapers reported the blowups in great detail, but that did not seem to stop the races. Even the passengers knew about the danger, but seemed to care little. When a race took place, one could see all the passengers on deck cheering their boat on to win the race!

You be Miss Muffin's travel agent!

Miss Sarah Muffin is about to make a long journey from her home to the home of her married sister. The journey will take from three to five days to complete, depending on weather conditions.

Make up a game about Miss Muffin's travels. With the help of your atlas, decide from which place to which place Sarah will travel. Her trip will include the following:

- a carriage ride
- a voyage by bateau
- a day on a steamboat
- a stagecoach ride on a corduroy road and on a muddy road
- a ride by ox-cart
- one night each at two different inns
- one night at a farmer's house
- one night on a steamboat

From the information you have read in this book about the above ways of travel, make up two sets of cards. One set of cards should deal with good travel conditions; the other with travel difficulties. Make up at least ten of each. For example:
TRAVEL DIFFICULTY *Miss Muffin hits her head while leaning out of the stagecoach.* MISS ONE TURN!
GOOD CONDITION *It is a clear night. The steamboat glides along ahead of schedule.* MOVE AHEAD TWO SPACES!

The winner is the first one to reach Sarah's sister's house. To make the game more exciting, you can make 5-10 spaces on the board *Town squares.* Each time you land on one of these spaces, you can pick up one *Service card.* Each service card should take care of one or more TRAVEL DIFFICULTY. A service card must match the travel difficulty.
DIFFICULTY: *The stagecoach loses a wheel.*
SERVICE: *A stagecoach wheel is fixed by the wheelwright.*

Miss Sarah Muffin is now on board a steamboat. She wonders whether there will be a storm. She is traveling alone. Should she go below into the lounge filled with men? Should she open her umbrella and stick out the storm? What should she do?

The steamboat below had to travel through many locks to get to the lower level. Why do you think so many locks were necessary?

Canals, the water connection

The building of canals was another big step in improving water travel. Canals were built to detour around rapids or to link up bodies of water, such as lakes and rivers. People no longer had to portage or carry their boat around rapids or from a lake to a river. They could travel the whole route by water.

Today it is easy to build a canal with all the modern machinery that is available. In the days of the early settlers, it took thousands of people and horses to finish the task. The building of a canal took a lot of time. Horses were used to pull the giant scoops which dug out the earth. Huge root-pullers were used to pull up the stumps of the large trees that were in the way.

Often the lakes and rivers which the canals connected were on different levels. Canals had to be built so that boats could travel easily in both directions. A system of *locks* were put in to make travel in both directions possible. Locks are sections of canals with water-tight gates at each end. The gates open to let a boat in and to allow it to move to the next higher or the next lower section.

Moving up, moving down

Here is how a boat moves from a lower to an upper lock:

The boat enters the lower lock through the lower gate. The lower gate closes tightly behind the boat. Small holes called *wickets* are opened in the upper gate. Water flows through these raising the boat higher as more water comes in. When the boat is as high as the water in the higher level, the upper gates are opened and the boat moves through to the upper level.

To move from an upper to a lower level, the opposite is done. As the boat enters the upper lock, the gate is once again closed. The wickets are opened in the lower gate of the lock and the water flows out of the upper lock. The water level inside the lock gets lower and lower until it is at the same level as the lower lock. The lower gate then opens and the boat steams into the lower level.

The teacher from the nearby village school teaches a lesson on travel. She shows her class how the new system of waterways, called canals, can provide better travel for them.

Many boats were pulled through the canals by horses. Once they reached a lake, they were either sailed or moved along by oars or poles.

The wickets in the upper gate are open. The water flows through. Soon the boat will be raised to the next level and be on its way.

Most of the early bridges were made out of wood or stone. This wooden bridge was built on top of the original bridge, which was just a plank of wood placed across two rocks. The later bridge is big enough for wagons, carriages and pedestrians.

Blazing the trails

When an early settler had to make a long trip, he or she tried to do as much of it as possible by water. However, sometimes it was not possible to travel by water, so people had to go by land.

Often the early settlers had no horses or wagons. They had to walk to town to get supplies or to the grist mill to have their grain ground. There were often no roads in the early days, so the pioneers had to rely on the trails made by the Indians through the forest. People tried to help each other by marking the trees along trails so that others would not get lost. Trees were chipped or *blazed* with a hatchet. These marked trails were called *blazed trails*. In the winter so many people used the trails that the snowshoes left a definite packed-down trail to follow.

Stuck in the mud

Groups of settlers got together and made rough roads by chopping trees down on each side of the trails. This made the trails wider, but the road itself was not much better. It was bumpy and filled with tree stumps. In the spring and summer the roads were often muddy. Horses and wagons were stuck hopelessly in the wet, swampy ground.

To get around the mud problem, the settlers cut the trees that were chopped down around the trails into logs. The logs were split in half and laid flat-side down next to each other on the road. Sometimes whole logs were put down. Often the logs could not be placed right beside each other because of bumps or stumps in the ground. These loggy roads were called *corduroy roads* after the ribbed fabric.

Half-a-log, half-a-log, bump, bump, bump

Both people and horses hated corduroy roads. Often horses broke their legs as they slipped into the space between two logs. If the logs were not exactly side by side, horses could easily trip or get caught. Many horses were so afraid of corduroy roads that they stopped dead when they came to one. They had to be coaxed slowly, one step at a time.

People wrote accounts of their trips on corduroy roads. One man described his journey as follows:

Some of the earliest bridges were also built using the corduroy method. Logs, secured in the bottom of the lake, held up long planks of wood. Whole or half logs were then put side-by-side across, forming a very bumpy bridge.

"The roads were so bad that no words can give an idea of them. We often sank in mud-holes; then over trunks of trees laid across swamps, called corduroy roads, where my poor bones dislocated. A wheel here and there, or a broken shaft lying on the roadside, told of former wrecks and disasters.

...When I arrived at Blandford my hands were swelled and blistered by continually grasping with all my strength an iron bar in the front of my vehicle to prevent myself from being flung out."

Plank roads were a big improvement over corduroy roads. If there happened to be a sawmill in the area, logs were taken there to be cut into planks or boards. These planks, laid side by side, made the roads less bumpy and much safer.

Each farmer was required by law to build a road in front of his or her house. Some did just that. Others, however, got together and built a fine network of roads for the good of the whole community. When people in an area worked together, that community became a much more enjoyable one in which to live.

The earth in the forest and in the towns was often muddy and swampy. The road-builders, as well as the travelers of the roads sank into the mud in wet weather.

29

Sydney Swift has taken Miss Muffin for a ride in his sleigh. They arrive at the tollgate. Will Sydney Swift pay? Will he swiftly slide past the tollgate keeper? Will Sydney demand a kiss from Miss Muffin as her part of the toll payment? What do you expect Sydney to do?

Toll roads

During times of war many more roads were built because it was necessary for soldiers to get from one place to another quickly and safely. Even in times of peace many roads were built by soldiers. If a private company paid for the building of a road, a tollgate was put up at both ends of the finished road. People had to pay to use the road. The money was then used to keep the road in good repair. However, much of the toll money went into the pockets of the toll-gate keepers. People knew this. Often angry, they refused to pay. Many dashed through the gate without paying, as the tollgate keeper ran screaming and yelling after them.

Rules of the road

There were few traffic rules in the days of the early settlers. Below are some of the ones we found. From looking at old pictures it is easy to see that few people obeyed or even knew about traffic laws!

- Wagons and buggies must use two or more bells on their harnesses.
- Drivers must keep to the right side of the roadway.
- Wagons may not park on town streets for any longer than 24 hours.
- Cattle and sheep must stay off public roads. (However, in some cities pigs were let loose at five o'clock in the morning to eat the garbage off the roads.)
- Driving at unreasonable speeds is not allowed
- Settlers must mark roads near their property with trees or branches.
- Settlers must clear snowdrifts from their roads in winter.

Many people did not pay the tollhouse keepers. These fellows not only run past, but one even thumbs his nose at the keeper.

It certainly seems that the drivers in this picture have forgotten the rules of the road. These pedestrians would not dare cross without the help of the friendly policeman.

Frank Church, nineteenth century artist, drew this picture to show how important animals were to people in those days. Why would each of these animals be important to the early settlers? Which ones could be used for travel? Why do you think Church included the stork in his picture?

Farmers relied on horses and oxen to take them to market, to the village store, and to the nearby grist mill. Without animals, survival in those early days was very difficult, if not impossible.

Beasts of burden

Animals were very important to the early settler. Not only were they a source of food, they were also the main means of travel. Horses and oxen were used to pull carts, buggies, wagons and sleighs of all sorts. Being without a horse or an ox in the wilderness made it nearly impossible to survive. Sometimes pioneers lived too far away from a village to be able to walk to it. Without the tools and supplies that were available at the general store, life was very difficult. It is no wonder that horse-stealing was treated so seriously! Horse-thieves were often hanged because they made someone else's life almost unbearable.

In the old days doctors did not usually see their patients in an office. Most doctors made house-calls then. Without horses, doctors would not have been able to reach their sick patients in time.

Many types of animals were used for pulling carriages and carts. Horses and oxen were the most popular. However, this young man had neither. Because every young person has the urge to travel, our little friend harnessed his chicken to get him to his destination. Will his chicken be too "chicken" to cross the road?

Dog-trains, such as the one in this old painting, were used in the north for pulling sleighs and carioles. These dogs are decorated with bells. What season must it be?

This early service station was one of many stops on a stagecoach's journey. Instead of selling gasoline, it allowed horses to refuel on hay and water. It provided a resting place for horses. Tired horses were replaced by fresh ones on each new stage of the journey.

Caring for the animals

Today we have gas stations to fuel and service our cars. In the days of the early settlers, horses and wagons also had to be serviced. Horses needed food and water. It was usually not difficult to feed animals, as there were plenty of places for grazing on a journey. If a settler went to town there was usually a place where animals could be fed and watered. Often there were drinking troughs right in the streets.

Most of the larger inns and taverns had stables located behind them. There horses could rest after a long journey. Often tired horses were exchanged for fresh ones at the inns. Stagecoach drivers exchanged their horses regularly because their journeys were usually long ones.

Instead of streetcars, horses and oxen were a common sight on early city roads.

In many small communities the blacksmith shop was right at the home of the blacksmith. While the horses got new shoes and repairs were made to the sleigh, these settlers enjoy some tea with the family of the blacksmith. Because many people visited the blacksmith regularly, the blacksmith shop was a good place to catch up on the latest village news.

The travel service team

The animals, such as horses, oxen and mules, that were used for carrying or pulling needed shoes to protect their hoofs. The *blacksmith* made the horse-shoes and nailed them onto the animal's hoofs. These shoes had to be changed often.

Because of bad road conditions, wagon wheels and axles were often damaged. The person who looked after broken or damaged wheels was the *wheelwright*.

The *harness-maker* was another member of the travel service team. Pioneers needed harnesses, straps and whips. The harnesses and straps were for securing wagons to horses and oxen. Whips were used to make animals go faster.

Horses go through many horseshoes while traveling. Elizabeth hammers out a new one.

After a bit of hoof-filing, the horse above is ready for another rough trip.

Wheelwrights fixed broken wheels and other carriage parts. Because of bad road conditions, wheelwrights were busy.

Blacksmiths shod both horses and oxen. Animals were held steady, as shown below, while the shoes were nailed on.

The harness-maker made harnesses and whips and sold the bells which were used to decorate the horses.

These pioneers are traveling to their new homestead in a conestoga wagon. Father will now chop some wood for a fire so that the family can eat lunch. Mother rests a spell and puffs on her pipe while the children get the food from the wagon.

The Conestoga wagon

Conestoga wagons were most commonly used to transport freight and settlers. These wagons were first built by German pioneers who settled in Pennsylvania. They were later used all over North America.

The Conestoga wagon was especially suitable for pioneer travel. The wheels were large so that the wagon was high off the ground. The bottom of the wagon did not hit the stumps and rocks on the road. The wagon could even cross shallow rivers without getting wet. The body of the wagon was curved slightly lower in the middle. This curve kept the freight in the middle. It prevented goods from falling out or from shifting from one end of the wagon to another. Conestoga wagons were usually painted in bright colors.

There was often a small stove inside the wagon to warm the family. The stovepipe stuck out of the canvas top. Horses or oxen pulled Conestoga wagons. The wagons moved slowly because the roads were so rough. Sometimes the milk carried by the pioneers was churned into butter by the end of the journey because the wagon shook so much.

The driver of the wagon sat over the left wheel. The wagons pulled slightly to the right. When the settlers came over from Europe, they were used to traveling on the left side of the road. Because the Conestoga wagons pulled to the right, people began to drive on the right hand side of the road in North America.

A family of mother, father and son is looking after this pack-train for their neighbors and friends. The goods are being taken to market and will be traded for other goods and supplies needed by the members of the community.

Pack trains

With land travel being so difficult, it was a challenge to get produce from the farm to the market. If there was a general store nearby, many of the pioneers took their produce there. The storekeeper then had to transport the goods to market. Some farmers, however, preferred to take their produce to a big town or city market.

Each fall groups of farmers got together and organized pack-trains to town. Only a few people were needed to make the journey. The master driver led the horses, which were packed down with produce. The others watched the horses behind. The train traveled by day and rested by night. The horses were *hobbled* so that they would not run away. A *hobble* was a short rope tied between the two front legs of a horse to keep it from running away, while it allowed horses to walk to grazing spots.

Each horse had a bell around its neck. The strikers of the bells were tied when the horses were on the trail. However, when the train neared the town, they were untied. The ringing bells anounced the arrival of the pack-train. The expression "going to town with bells on" started with the pack trains.

Some pack trains were made up of oxen and wagons or carts. Red River carts, drawn either by horses or oxen, were common in western freighting.

Once the freighters traded their produce for other supplies, they prepared to head back with their newly-bought goods. On the way back, farmers were often held up by robbers for their supplies or money. It was a custom for farmers to meet at a tavern and travel home together. That way they had a better chance to arrive safely.

The pack-train has arrived safely to town. The produce has been sold and new supplies bought. These two farmers pass the time playing cards and drinking while they wait for a few more traveling companions. Traveling home in groups was much safer then.

It is a beautiful day for stagecoach travel. These nineteenth century passengers are enjoying the scenic mountain route the driver has taken.

Stagecoaches

As more roads were built, there were more types of wagons and carriages to travel over them. Stagecoaches started to carry people from town to town.

Early stagecoaches were not designed for comfort. Instead of shock-absorbers or springs, these coaches were held up by leather straps. These straps did not absorb any of the shocks from the bumps in the road. The passenger cabin of a stagecoach held nine persons. There were two rows of seats facing forward and one row facing back. Five more people could sit on top of the coach. Some of the baggage was put inside the coach with the passengers. The rest was strapped onto the back and the top of the coach.

The first coaches had only one entrance. It was located over the driver's seat. The passengers had to crawl over the other benches to get to their seats. There were no backs on the benches, so people had to sit up without any support for their backs. After many days of traveling like this,

people were very tired and in bad spirits. It was not strange to find that people who traveled together hated each other by the end of the trip!

Stagecoach travelers faced many problems. Roads were terrible in most places and there was always a chance that a stage would overturn. If the driver suspected that the stage might tip over, he called to the passengers to lean to one side. Sometimes the passengers had to hang right out of the windows in order to keep the coach upright. If a tree was near the road when the passengers were hanging out, there was a good chance of someone getting a rather large bump on the head.

Stagecoach drivers were called "coachmen." Most coachmen were rough and ready characters. They had to face so many dangers trip after trip that they often became reckless. They drove too fast in order to arrive at the next town on time. They did not care much about the comfort of their passengers.

Robberies were as common as stagecoaches in the days of the early settlers. These passengers may be robbed more than once during their long journey. The bandits loved to rob mail coaches because many of the letters carried money.

Carrying the mail

Many stagecoaches were also mail coaches. Mail was delivered to the general store of each community about once a week. The driver announced the arrival of the coach by blowing a horn. The stage stopped for about half an hour. The passengers had a chance to stretch their legs during this time. The driver changed horses and collected the outgoing mail. Because letters sometimes contained money, highway robberies often occurred.

Wagons and coaches were often changed into sleighs in winter. The wheels were removed and runners were put on. Passengers got smoother rides as soon as the roads were covered with snow.

Staging the journey

Passenger coaches were called *stagecoaches* because the driver had to change horses about every 24 kilometers. The distance between two stops was called a *stage* of the journey. Stagecoaches were usually used for long journeys. *Stagewagons* were used for shorter trips from town to town.

Stagewagons were nothing more than farmers' wagons. They were open with one or two planks of wood placed from side to side to serve as seats. One or two horses pulled a stagewagon. Stagewagons used back roads, while stagecoaches used main roads.

This old mail coach ran on wheels in the summer and on runners in winter. It carried passengers inside and out. The settler on top is taking his produce to market. The passenger in the back is taking his nap.

Sunday was the day for carriage rides in the city and country. Many young men and fashionable young ladies paraded through the streets on Sunday afternoons. It was a custom to have the horses groomed, the carriages polished, and to wear one's best clothes. The ladies on top of the carriages carried parasols to protect themselves from the hot sun.

The streets of this city are packed with sleighs, cutters, horses and people. These Sunday drivers must find it difficult to get anywhere with so much traffic around.

Sunday drivers

Most farmers had wagons or carts that they or a craftsman in the community had built. When settlers grew more wealthy, they could afford to buy the buggies and carriages built in the larger towns and cities. Many fine carriages were advertised in the papers.

Buggies, gigs and shays usually had two wheels and were pulled by one horse. They had tops which could be pulled up or folded down like the tops of convertible cars. Buggies were used to carry people, not goods. Settlers used buggies for going to church and for visiting friends. Horse-drawn carriages were larger. They usually had four wheels. Several horses pulled the larger carriages. As some settlers grew wealthy, they could afford larger, fancier and more comfortable carriages.

People liked to go for carriage rides on Sundays. It was a way of showing off to friends. People used to show off new clothes, new girlfriends and boyfriends, new husbands and wives, and, of course, new horses and carriages. People showed off by racing their carriages, shays, gigs, buggies and sleighs. They showed off by parading through town and city streets. Traffic jams were already a problem on Sunday afternoons. Pedestrians were often afraid to cross the streets on Sundays. Parks were also filled with carriages or sleighs, depending on the time of year.

Hundreds of wagons dot the western plains.

Westward bound

As more settlers came from Europe, many of the grown children of the earlier settlers decided to move west or north to get more land. Many Mormon settlers from Minnesota, for example, moved north-west to Alberta by wagon train. When a group of people decided to move west, they organized a wagon train. People felt it was safer to travel in large groups than to travel alone. As many as two hundred wagons made up a wagon train. Scouts traveled ahead to choose a place for camp. When the others caught up, the wagon train formed a large circle for protection. Horses were *hobbled* (see p.39) and then set out to graze. The travelers gathered wood or dried buffalo chips with which they made fires. People sat around the fires, cooked their food, talked, sang and told stories. They went to bed early and were ready to roll again by four in the morning. It took people months to reach their new homes.

Wagon trains were divided into groups of four wagons. If these wagons broke off from the main train, they would still be able to survive. Both horses and oxen were used for westward travel. However, oxen were considered much better. They were stronger, needed less food and water and they could be eaten if necessary. Experienced wagon train guides often refused to lead people who wanted to make their journey by horse.

The pioneers who traveled across the prairies to the Rockies found that their old ways of travel were often not suitable for the west. Here are some illustrations of the new ways these settlers found to travel long, flat, high, and rocky distances.

The town is filled with excitement as the wagons roll in.

Who needs snow when the land is so flat?

Cross-country skiis were excellent for mountainous western winter travel.

Sailing on sand? Well, why not, if that's all you've got!

Sure-footed donkeys are best suited for mountain travel. But are they stubborn!

Sleighs, cutters, carioles and stagecoaches were everywhere in winter. People saved up

Streets filled with sleighs

As soon as the pioneers were settled, their need to travel grew even greater. People needed to be part of a community. Settlers needed supplies and services provided by others. Most of all, they needed other people.

Winter was the best time to travel. It was also the best time for settlers to socialize. The harvest was finished, the pantries were full and there was not much work to be done.

Roads or paths were usually covered with

their important trips as well as their social calls until there was snow on the ground.

snow. It was easy to glide over the smooth surface. People traveled in sleighs, cutters, carioles and sometimes on toboggans pulled by dogs. They went to parties, visited friends and made long trips to the homes of relatives.

The early sleighs in which people traveled were nothing more than boxes on runners.

The later sleighs and cutters were beautifully made. They had soft seats and fur lining. During the Christmas season horses were decorated with bells and bright ribbons. Land travel became enjoyable and romantic. For some people, it was an opportunity for sport. Settlers were constantly challenging each other to races in the snow.

Miss Muffin's date with Captain Buzbie

Miss Sarah Muffin has an exciting date with one of the best-looking men in her sister's town. Captain Buzbie has asked her to go tobogganing at a nearby hill. He promises a day of thrills, chills and unexpected spills. Shall we join them on their fun-filled day?

They arrive at the huge hill in front of Montmorency Falls. They climb up with great difficulty. Sliding down is easier, but much more dangerous!

Night has fallen. Captain Buzbie has somehow lost his way. He would like very much to know where they are!

Some helpful farmers lead Captain Buzbie out of his unfortunate predicament.

Just as the sun comes up, they are home at last! Will Miss Muffin go out with Captain Buzbie again? Do you think he kept his promise about the chills, thrills and spills?

Hustle, bustle, dash and scurry! At Christmas, everyone's in a hurry. The price they pay for not being slow, most often is a quick roll in the snow.

The hazards of snow and ice

Although winter was by far the best time to travel, settlers still faced many difficulties on their trips. Snowdrifts were so high, that sometimes it was impossible to get over or around them. Sleighs were often overturned. The many reckless drivers on the roads caused problems for themselves and others. Sudden blizzards and snowstorms often made travel impossible. Travelers who were caught in these storms sometimes did not survive their trip.

Traveling over frozen lakes was a dangerous gamble. Sometimes parts of the ice melted under the snow and down would go the horse and sleigh without warning. People were ready for many of these possible disasters. If a horse and sleigh fell into a lake, a rope was immediately put around the neck of the horse to keep water from getting into its lungs. The horse would then float and be pulled out safely.

To save this horse, one must act quickly and tie a rope around its neck. That way the horse will stay afloat and survive.

One of the hazards of winter travel was the extremely cold weather. People traveled in open sleighs. If they lost their way, they arrived at their destinations with a nasty frostbite.

The sudden blizzard

On this drear night, going whither,
Mournful Mother, with thy child?
What sad fate has brought thee hither,
Now the snow-storm, sweeping wild,
Buries every path and track,
And the night is gathering black?

All the firs are weighed with snow;
Every hedge heaves like a grave.
Faster o'er the road you go
Spreads the white and treacherous wave
After thee, with silent tread,
Steals a summoner from the dead.

Clasp thy child unto thy breast,
Closer, lest he tear it hence.
Onward; if thou stay and rest
For a moment, by yon fence,
Yon pursuer's savage grasp
Thy fond treasure will unclasp.

Hurry, while thy chilling blood
Still can give thee life and speed;
Knee-deep through the freezing flood,
Faster o'er the buried mead;
Till the distant village peal
O'er thy drowsy senses steal.

Then there come a pleasant jangling,
As of bells, and lusty voices;
And a shouting, merry wrangling --
Ere she leaps up and rejoices,
Two great giant-arms have bound her.
'Tis her husband who has found her!
(1870)

Sudden storms were the enemy of every traveler. This mother, father and child are in the middle of a prairie storm. Thunder and lightning threaten. Rivers form from all the rain.

Even trains could not always guarantee a safe journey. This one went off its tracks.

This traveler took the holdup into his own hands. He tackled the bandit!

When this coach came to a sudden stop, the driver tried his best to get the horses moving again. Nothing worked! Suddenly a flash of lightning lit up the sky! The driver saw a big hole where the bridge used to be. The horses saved the lives of all the passengers!

Travel troubles

Even today when people travel they take risks in doing so. We hear of many car accidents and plane crashes. However, in the days of early travel, it was more unusual to have a safe journey than a difficult one. Passengers in coaches often arrived with aching backs and bumps and bruises, if they were lucky. Sometimes broken bones were a part of stagecoach travel. More often than not, coaches were robbed by highway bandits. People usually carried cash when they traveled.

Bad weather was always one of the traveler's worst enemies. There were no heated cars to keep people warm or out of the snow and rain. Often it was difficult to find shelter in a sudden storm. People arrived with colds and pneumonia.

Bridges were worn away by time and weather and sometimes passengers fell into the waters below as they tried to cross.

The ship's last passenger is saved!

City streets were tied up with traffic, even in the early days. This horse traveled too far without a rest. It fell down from exhaustion and had to be carried away.

City travel

Early streetcars were pulled by horses or mules, not powered by electricity. These passengers are proud to have their pictures taken aboard this new form of transportation.

And this was one of the better roads! All that fresh, delicious bread will have to go to waste. These fellows are stranded in a sea of mud without a horse or wheels.

It is hard to imagine a city tied up in a bicycle traffic jam, but here is one right before our eyes. No matter how people traveled, they always found a way to create traffic jams!

Not all inns and taverns were as fancy as the one in the above picture. Some were just log cabins in the forest. Farmers also took travelers in for the night for a modest fee. This first class hotel has stables in the back for tired horses. Much of the food served at this inn is grown in the fields right beside it. How many rooms do you think there are inside? What kind of people would stay at such a hotel?

Inns and taverns

When people traveled they had three choices of where to spend their nights. One could camp out in the wilderness, put up at an inn or stay at a farmhouse. Many of the forest inns were nothing more than one-room log houses. Even the larger inns were not very comfortable. As many as ten people often slept in one room. Lice and bedbugs were constant companions in the straw beds. Most inns provided one comb or brush for all the guests to use. A pig trough was the only place for washing up. Some of the bigger inns had outhouses, but most did not. Guests had to tramp out into the bush in the middle of the night.

Grab your grub

A breakfast bell rang early in the morning. Everyone ran from his or her bed for food.

When an inn was located near a village or town, it became the social center of that community. These villagers got carried away with their merrymaking!

Once it was gone, there were no seconds (or firsts if you were slow). There was no choice in what one could eat. The innkeeper usually served only one kind of food. Everyone grabbed the food and ate quickly. Table manners were not popular. People just shoved the food into their mouths as quickly as they could so they wouldn't miss out.

Merrymaking

In a small village or community, the inn was the center of social life. People gathered there for parties and dances. Often a lot of drinking took place. In some cases this led to violence. People who are drunk often can not control their emotions and want to fight with others. Regulations were passed in most communities. Bars had to be closed Sundays. In the evenings taverns often closed at 9 in the winter and 10 in the summer.

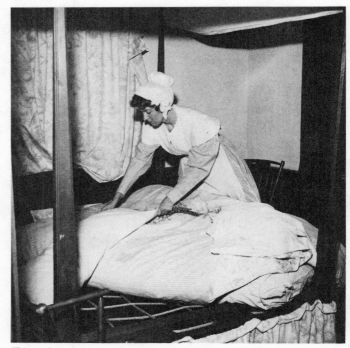

The beds at this inn are made of wood and rope. The mattress is made of straw. The innkeeper changes the sheets weekly.

In the early days there were few machines. Building a railroad meant work for many people. Engineers were sent ahead to survey the land through which the tracks would go. These men set up camp and went out on snowshoes to explore the land.

The railroad changed small villages such as the one above into busy, booming towns.

The railroad opens the west

The railway opened the west to new settlers. There was a lot of good farmland in the west. Much of the good farmland in the east was already taken by earlier settlers. The railway ended loneliness for many people. A person could now more easily visit relatives and friends. Small communities could get supplies from larger towns and cities. Young people could travel to the cities for better jobs and higher education. Inland towns grew quickly into large cities because the railroad made inland trade possible. Goods could be transported quickly and easily by train.

It took many thousands of people to build a railway. Tracks had to be built over mountains and rivers as well as through forests. Each track had two steel rails which were fastened by spikes and metal plates to wooden ties. Little gaps were left between the ends of rails. Because steel expands in heat, the gaps between the rails stopped the rails from buckling up on hot days. The clicking sound that trains make is a result of the steel wheels going over the gaps. Rails were laid over crushed rock. The rock held the ties in place, kept grass from growing and allowed water to drain.

Trains were sometimes called land yachts *because they offered passengers comfortable travel.*

Every mode of transportation had its faults. Even though the train was by far the best way to travel, it too had its problems. In the picture above a man runs to warn the engineer about the danger ahead. The middle picture on the opposite page shows the difficulties early trains met with in winter. Even the attached snowplow can not budge all that snow. Derailments and collisions (bottom right) were the biggest danger, costing many lives.

The not-quite-perfect-train

The railroad joined settlements in the east and west into one country. It allowed people to move around for better land, education and jobs. Before the railroad, people had to make big travel plans. They had to have a lot of free time in order to get to where they were going. With the coming of the train, people did not have to make long-range plans to visit friends or relatives. Trains made for better travel and better travel made for better lives.

However, trains were far from perfect. The first rails were made from wood. The wood was covered with metal. Wooden rails were dangerous because often an end would come loose, curl up and come through the floor of the train. Some people were badly injured by these *sneakheads* or curled ends.

Trains often derailed. Broken tracks went unnoticed until too late. Trains collided. Sometimes two trains, heading toward each other, used the same track and neither engineer knew about the other train. Though not perfect, trains were still by far the best way to go anywhere!

The DeWitt Clinton, one of North America's earliest trains.

Wouldn't a horse and sleigh be a welcome sight right about now?

Will these people take the train again?

A peddler in a horse and carriage comes to the rescue of this young couple. Their new "horseless carriage" has run out of gas in the middle of the country. Although automobiles were new and exciting, they too had their share of problems. There was no gas gauge to show how much gas was left. Often it was difficult to start cars, as there was no starter or key to turn. Instead, a crank-handle was located on the outside front of the car.

New sources of energy

Most of the modern travel discoveries, such as the railroad, automobile and airplane, were made in or after the nineteenth century. For hundreds of years people depended on wind and animals for their travel. Suddenly, many new sources of energy were discovered and these new fuels powered the new inventions.

We are again coming to an age in which new sources of energy are needed. Cars, trains and planes are constantly being improved. We have even found a way to travel regularly into space. What will happen, however, when all the fuel runs out? Will we have to come back down to earth and hitch horses in front of our automobiles? Will we be pioneers in a brand new era of travel?

When a car stopped in town, people gathered around to have a closer look at the marvelous machine. These boys will probably own one when they grow up.